Original title:
Tasting Summer

Copyright © 2025 Creative Arts Management OÜ
All rights reserved.

Author: Harris Montgomery
ISBN HARDBACK: 978-1-80586-306-9
ISBN PAPERBACK: 978-1-80586-778-4

The Warmth of Culminating Eves

When the sun spills lemonade skies,
Sipping joy while my ice cream flies.
Bugs on a mission, buzzing for fun,
Diving for desserts, oh where's my bun?

Picnic ants sneak home with my fries,
Under the blanket, my surprise dies!
The soft breeze teases my napkin fleet,
While ketchup rivers run wild at my feet.

Symphony of Seasonal Sweets

Whipped cream clouds dance on my spoon,
Chocolate raindrops make me croon.
Strawberries giggle as they play tag,
Melons roll by, oh what a wag!

Popsicles melt, create a splash,
I'm dodging drips in a crazy dash.
Cookies crumble with laughter and cheer,
A sugary chorus brings everyone near.

Caramelized Sunshine

Golden drizzles on my cheeky grin,
Like sticky fingers, where to begin?
Marshmallows roasting, a campfire's light,
S'more stacked tall, what a glorious sight!

Chocolate oozing, a molten surprise,
Marshmallow clouds floating in my eyes.
Droopy ice cream cones tempt fate,
Dripping tales that can't wait to sate.

Bliss from the Orchard

Apples giggle as they tumble down,
Plucking laughter instead of frown.
Peaches and cherries wave from the tree,
Inviting all, "Come enjoy with me!"

Cider bubbling with a fizzy cheer,
Grass stains grow bold in the summer sphere.
Smiles ripple through the fruity feast,
Nature's candy makes joy increased.

Joys of the Heat

The sun is out, what a sight,
Sweat beads glisten, very bright.
Ice cream drips down my chin,
Oh, summer sun, where to begin?

Popsicles melt with sunny glee,
Yellow lemonade calls to me.
Flip-flops flapping, kids all scream,
Floating in pools, living the dream!

Refreshing Reflections

Water balloons in mid-air,
Giggles and shouts everywhere.
Sunshine burns, the grass is hot,
Someone forgot that sunscreen spot.

Shade beneath a leafy tree,
Sipping drinks, just you and me.
Lemon zest and mint collide,
Give my thirst a summer ride!

Chocolate and Cherry Sunsets

The ice cream truck's jingle rings,
Chocolate sprinkles, oh the things!
Cherry red sunsets make me smile,
Sticky hands, we sit a while.

Messy faces, laughter loud,
Soft serve towers, like a cloud.
When the day fades, so divine,
Summer's treat, the stars align!

Ages of Golden Sips

On a porch, with drink in hand,
Sippin' sunshine, oh so grand.
Cousins argue who's the best,
As grandpa snores, take a rest.

Fizzy drinks and fruity puffs,
Poolside snacks, who's had enough?
In the stillness, laughter flows,
Golden sips that summer shows!

Glimmering Hours of Citrus Light

Lemonade stands invade the street,
Popsicles dribble, oh what a treat!
Kids chase after, drinks in their hands,
Every sip bursts like marching bands.

Sunburn sings on our silly skin,
Sunscreen wars, where to begin?
Orange slices in a playful fight,
Juicy laughter fills the bright twilight.

Harvest Songs Under a Blue Sky

Baskets of berries, a colorful mess,
Raspberry juice stains every dress.
Giggles ripple in the warm breeze,
Nature's jam, oh how it pleases!

Silly hats perched, each one a crown,
Bee stings gossip as we settle down.
Swatting flies like skillful pros,
'This is summer' each friend knows!

Dancing in the Sunbeams

Sunlight twirls on the grass so green,
Flip-flops flying in a sunny scene.
Chasing shadows, we let out a cheer,
Bouncing around like we've no fear!

Picnic blankets as our weekend throne,
Sandwiches sharing secrets unknown.
Kites tug gently against the air,
As we burst into giggles everywhere.

Melon Winks and Golden Tints

Watermelon smiles line up in a row,
Juicy bites bring a sensational glow.
Spitting seeds like a champion sport,
While friends gather for a fruity report.

Ice cream drips, a colorful mess,
Chocolate sprinkles in glorious excess.
Silly faces with sticky balloons,
Summer fun played under the moon.

Dance of the Summer Spirits

In gardens bright, the spirits sway,
With lemonade laughs, they dance all day.
Jellybean shoes and ice cream hats,
They tango with bees and giggling cats.

A pirate ship made of beachside sand,
With gummy sharks, oh, isn't it grand?
They spin in circles, oh what a sight,
As marshmallow clouds float by in delight.

Evening Strolls with Tangy Treats

As twilight paints the sky in gold,
We wander paths where stories are told.
Popcorn explosions, a buttery blast,
While fireflies twinkle, oh how they last!

Cotton candy stuck to our noses,
We laugh at the sweetness, the fun it poses.
Lemonade rivers, we splash with glee,
Bouncing like bunnies, so wild and free!

Sunshine's Sweet Rhapsody

Balloons in hand, we leap and cheer,
As watermelon smiles bring us near.
Sunbeams tickle, oh what a game,
Chasing shadows, all feeling the same.

Bubble gum dreams float past our ears,
Laughter erupts; it's the best of years.
With cupcakes dancing on paper plates,
We toast to joy and sweet summer fates.

Crickets' Ambrosial Chorus

Crickets sing with a zestful flair,
While ice pops drip, without a care.
A chorus of giggles fills the night air,
As anchor racks of snacks, we repair.

The s'mores are melting with marshmallow glee,
Sticky fingers, just you and me.
Firelight flickers, a warm embrace,
In the dance of flavors, we find our place.

Dappled Sunlight Through Leafy Canopies

In the glade, laughter flies,
Squirrels dance and tease the skies.
Sunbeams play on peanut jars,
Chasing shadows, counting stars.

A picnic blanket blooms anew,
With sandwiches and soda too.
Ants march in with tiny flair,
Claiming crumbs beyond compare.

Friends giggle, dodging bees,
Clumsy moves, then tumbles, whee!
Each sunbeam a playful wink,
As juice spills and torrents sink.

The Crunch of Grilled Corn on Cob

On the grill, the sizzle sings,
Butter drips like summer wings.
Laughter bursts around the fire,
Each kernel fuels the fun, inspires.

With every bite, a sweet delight,
Face transformed, a comical sight.
Juicy dribbles slide and smear,
Charged with giggles, full of cheer.

Corn husk crowns upon our heads,
Who's the king? A cob affair spreads!
Chasing down a runaway ear,
Grilled delights bring joy and cheer.

Balmy Breezes Carrying Sweet Hues.

The wind whispers soft and warm,
Giggling leaves, a playful charm.
Skirts twirl like ice cream cones,
While happy voices dance in tones.

A kite misbehaves, takes flight,
Chasing clouds, a silly sight.
Ice pops rocket, colors bright,
Sticky fingers, sheer delight.

We chase the breeze, we run and glide,
Frolicking on the summertime tide.
Lemonade spills, a fruity mess,
Yet in this chaos, we find blessedness.

Beneath the Sun's Embrace

Lazing under skies of blue,
Each moment feels like a debut.
Faces glisten, laughter frees,
Funnies shared in perfect ease.

The hammock sways, a gentle ride,
Tickling toes, the sun's warm side.
A book in hand, then a nap—
Dreams of snacks and a sun-kissed map.

Chasing shadows, playing tag,
Silly dances, playful brag.
Beneath the sun, we find our zest,
In hilarity, we feel our best.

Cherries Hanging in Harmony

A cherry tree filled with glee,
Dancing with wind like an acrobat.
Birds plot schemes for a juicy spree,
While squirrels snicker, 'Just look at that!'

Red fruit glistens under the sun,
As the branches bow with a laugh.
It's a chase when the kids all run,
But who'll get the last, juicy half?

Sunflower Fields of Flavor

In yellow seas where bees do buzz,
Sunflowers wink at the skies so blue.
They chuckle softly, making a fuzz,
While sipping nectar, just like you do.

Kites tangle up in the swaying blooms,
As children skate through paths of gold.
Each twist and turn brings out wild zooms,
While parents chase dreams of the bold.

Afternoon Delights on the Path

Ice cream cones tumble down the lane,
Melted puddles create a surprise.
Giggles echo through sunshine and rain,
As sticky fingers paint sweetened skies.

Lemonade stands flaunt their sweet charms,
With kids lined up, hands full of change.
Sipping sunshine in icy arms,
Plans of mischief in every range.

The Essence of Warmth

Barbecues hum with sizzling cheer,
While friends argue over the best spice.
The laughter grows louder, time slips near,
As burgers play dodgeball, think twice!

Firefly dances light into dusk,
As marshmallows roast, each bite a dream.
Echoes of joy, a vivid husk,
Where friendship is dessert, supreme.

Spirited Sips of Bliss

A glass of lemonade so bright,
With lipstick prints, it's quite a sight.
I raise a toast to cherry pies,
While squirrels dance beneath the skies.

The ice cream truck plays a silly tune,
Chasing kids like a big balloon.
Each creamy scoop, a vibrant swirl,
We laugh as sticky fingers twirl.

Craving the Warmth

Barefoot on the sunlit grass,
The neighbor's dog runs by so fast!
With every splash from the garden hose,
We giggle as the chaos grows.

A picnic spread with ants in tow,
Hot dogs bouncing in a row.
Who needs a diet, it's a feast,
We'll diet later, to say the least!

Lush Landscapes of Flavor

Mango slices, juicy and sweet,
A sticky nightmare, oh what a treat!
Berries plucked from bushes near,
We munch with laughter, never fear.

The BBQ smoke fills the air,
With friends who run, without a care.
Between the bites and jokes we share,
Sun-kissed memories light the fair.

Cups Overflowing with Summertime Joys

A jug of punch that overflows,
With fruit confetti, goodness shows.
We dance like crazy, cups in hand,
As laughter bubbles, oh so grand.

Sunshine spills like melted gold,
Reminders of the tales retold.
We sip and sing, our spirits high,
As fireflies twinkle in the sky.

Rustic Picnics and Forgotten Notes

We spread a blanket, so wide, so grand,
With ants and crumbs, a strange band.
Forgotten sandwiches, half-eaten fries,
We're all just laughing under blue skies.

A picnic basket wearing a hat,
It caught the breeze, away it sat.
Chasing a kite that needs a friend,
In this chaos, the fun won't end.

Breezy Days of Lemonade Rivers

Sipping sunshine in a plastic cup,
With every gulp, we hiccup and sup.
A river of lemonade flows so sweet,
Got sticky fingers, and sand in our feet.

We dip our toes in the cool stream,
It splashes back, like an orange dream.
Laughing loudly, the day slips away,
With echoes of joy in the sun's last ray.

Honeyed Whispers in the Garden

Bees buzz by, the flowers sing,
In the garden, sweet chaos is king.
We chase butterflies with giggles and glee,
Honeyed secrets between you and me.

Tomatoes dancing, reaching for light,
We play hide-and-seek until night.
The veggies chuckle at our silly game,
In this wonderland, nothing's the same.

The Taste of Adventure on Warm Skin

Splashing through puddles, the rain acts shy,
We run in circles, we jump, we fly.
A sunburned nose tells tales so bold,
As stories of mischief in sunlight unfold.

With ice cream drips running down our chins,
We race the breeze, it giggles and spins.
Every summer day feels like a win,
With laughter echoing, let the fun begin!

Sun-Drenched Berries

Juicy gems from nature's hand,
A berry feast, oh, isn't it grand?
Squished between fingers, oh what a mess,
Nature's confetti, I must confess!

Strawberry smiles, blueberry grins,
Happiness comes with all of their sins.
Raspberry giggles, bursting with cheer,
Wipe the juice off, it's summer, my dear!

Whispering Waves on Warm Sand

Sandy toes, oh what a sight,
The ocean whispers, day turns to night.
Seagulls laugh, swooping in fast,
Squirted with sand, memories cast!

Children build castles, up they rise,
A moat of giggles, reaching the skies.
Buckets of laughter, splashes galore,
Waves slyly tickle, always wanting more!

Zest of Long Days

Lemonade sips, on porches we sway,
A citrus burst, brightening the day.
Sunburned noses, with laughter we clash,
Chasing ice cream trikes, oh what a dash!

Fireflies dance, in the evening light,
With twinkling jars, we'll chase them tonight.
Summer's a jester, with tricks up its sleeve,
A giggling prankster, watch what you believe!

Melon Slices Under Sunlight

Melon chunks, oh such delight,
Juicy explosions, feel so right.
Splatters of pink on our cheeks and chins,
The fruit parade; let the games begin!

Seeds like confetti, flying in fun,
Spitting contests, who will outrun?
Shade of a tree, we lie back in bliss,
Laughter and melon, the perfect summer kiss!

Citrus Legends

Lemons bouncing on the lawn,
Grapefruits giggle, dusk till dawn.
Oranges steal the sun's bright show,
As limes roll by, quite full of glow.

Citric knights in peel and zest,
Slipping away, they think they're the best.
A blender's roar, a fruity fight,
What's a smoothie? Just pure delight!

The Chill After the Heat

Ice cream trucks, they prowl the street,
Chasing kids on sticky feet.
Frosty cones, oh what a tease,
Melting fast, oh do please freeze!

Popcycles popping like fireworks,
Sticky fingers, yeah, it's the perks.
A splash in pools, a dive to cheer,
Only to find, the bathroom's near!

Sweet Spoils of the Meadow

Honeybees and daisies dance,
Chasing bugs who dare to prance.
Strawberry jams in jars so bright,
Getting jammed up, what a sight!

Berries hanging, a sneaky snack,
Butterflies flutter on the track.
Nature's treats, they call our name,
In this wild, sticky, berry game!

Embracing Juicy Warmth

Watermelon splatters everywhere,
Seeds go flying, whom do we scare?
Sipping drinks with silly straws,
Catching laughs with summer's pause.

Picnic blankets spread with flair,
Ants in line as if they care.
Dancing around a tongue-twisting jam,
Under a sun, oh yes, we sham!

Chasing Fireflies at Dusk

In twilight's glow, they start to dance,
Little lights in a playful prance.
I run in circles, arms spread wide,
Tripping over grass, trying to glide.

A jar in hand, hopes packed inside,
Fireflies laughing, they try to hide.
"Catch us all!" they gleefully tease,
I'm just a kid, on summer's breeze.

Nectarine Dreams on Sunlit Skin

Juicy bites dribble down my chin,
The nectar drips, it's a sticky win.
Yellow globes that burst with cheer,
I wear the taste like summer gear.

Each slice a sunbeam, bright and sweet,
I chase the juice with dancing feet.
Spinning around in lazy delight,
The fruit's my party, morning to night.

Citrus Kisses in the Breeze

A zesty wink from oranges bright,
They play a trick in morning light.
Lemonade splashes, a fizzy cheer,
Sour faces turn sweet, oh dear!

With every sip, my giggles grow,
Tart on the tongue, a citrus show.
I wear a crown of limey zest,
Here's to the summer, we are blessed!

Serenade of Crickets at Twilight

As day gives way to chirping song,
Crickets rehearse, all night long.
They strum a tune, legs tapping fast,
My dance routine is quite the blast!

Under the stars, they croon away,
While I trip over my lack of sway.
Laughter bubbles, a nighttime cheer,
With every croak, summer is here!

Abrir las Puertas del Amanecer

Sunshine slips through the cracks,
Birds argue over breakfast snacks.
Pancakes fly from the sizzling pan,
As syrup smiles at the sleepy man.

Coffee's dancing in a mug,
While toast pops up with a happy shrug.
The cat plots mischief with a wink,
Espresso dreams, the perfect link.

Laughter mingles with the breeze,
As slippers chase the buzzing bees.
Morning stretches, yawns a while,
And the day begins with a silly smile.

A Symphony of Beachcomber's Finds

Shells are whispering secrets paint,
While seagulls strut with a hint of disdain.
Someone drops a sandwich at my feet,
Gulls gather 'round, like a hungry fleet.

Sandy toes in a flip-flop dance,
Watching waves take a goofy stance.
A crab with swagger, pinching air,
Struts past, oblivious to my stare.

Children dig with mighty pride,
Building castles, the tide's eager tide.
Ice cream drips, leaving sweet trails,
Laughter echoes through salty gales.

The Lushness of Green Fields

Meadow creatures plot their day,
A squirrel holds a nut ballet.
Grass tickles legs that skip and run,
While daisies laugh under the sun.

Cowboys chase butterflies that roam,
While sheep play tag like they're at home.
Each step a bounce, a giggle, a glee,
As frogs join in for a wild spree.

Farmers grumble at weeds that sprout,
Their stubborn foes, they dance about.
With every poke from the pitchfork's glance,
The fields erupt in a green romance.

Wildflower Sips of Innocence

Wildflowers bloom like chaotic dreams,
Buzzing bees in fuzzy teams.
Petals wave in a sunny hug,
While kids run wild with a joyous tug.

Puddles reflect their goofy pride,
As muddy shoes go for a slide.
A dandelion bursts, seeds take flight,
Innocent giggles, a pure delight.

Ladybugs parade in a delicate line,
While kids compete, who'll spot the vine?
Nature's laughter rings so clear,
With wildflower sips, we dance up here.

Golden Evenings and Cold Drinks

Lemonade spills down my chin,
Sweaty palms and boisterous grins.
Ice cubes clink like jolly bells,
In this heat, who needs hotels?

Chasing dreams in flip-flop dance,
The lawn chair creaks—what a chance!
My friends all gather, laugh and play,
While the sun drips gold, come what may.

Flavorful Laughter in the Air

Corn on the cob, kernels pop,
Butter drips without a stop.
Spicy salsa makes us cheer,
While we dance and drink our beer.

Watermelon seeds take flight,
We giggle under string lights bright.
Catch a slice, don't be too shy,
It's a slice of summer pie!

Sweetness of Ripening Fruit

Peaches blush with sunny cheer,
Messy faces, laughter near.
Juicy dribbles down my hands,
Sticky fingers, summer plans.

Strawberry wars, we take aim,
Tomato toss—now that's the game!
With every bite, we squeal and shout,
Is this a fruit fight? I'm not in doubt!

Sunsets Spilling Colorful Hues

Painting skies with hues so wild,
Each sunset speaks—the stars reviled.
Picnic blankets spread with flair,
We toast to chaos, laughs in air.

With s'mores and sparks all around,
We watch the firelight dance unbound.
As twilight hugs the night, we find,
Summer madness, laughter intertwined.

Crisp Apples and Temperate Breezes

Juicy bites and crunching sounds,
Laughter echoes round the grounds.
Silly hats and picnic spills,
Chasing friends up grassy hills.

Wobbling carts with snacks galore,
Finding ants, we laugh and roar.
Sunshine tickles our funny bones,
As we munch on fruit and scones.

Whispers caught in gentle gusts,
Air so sweet, it's full of trust.
Rolling laughter fills the space,
As we dance with reckless grace.

Crispness lingers in the air,
We joke about the weight we bear.
With full bellies and silly grins,
We leap like goats on playful spins.

Figs and Fireflies

Figs so ripe, they burst like dreams,
Under stars, we plot our schemes.
Fireflies flick, a winking show,
Counting flashes as they glow.

Tasting flavors rich and wild,
Giggles sound when summer's styled.
Every bite a squishy thrill,
Swallowing sweets, we've had our fill.

Chasing lights, we skip around,
In this gold, our joy is found.
Sticky fingers and bright eyes,
Tummy aches and laughter rise.

As the moon begins to sway,
We're just kids who love to play.
With figs in hand and hearts so free,
We laugh like we'll never flee.

Golden Nectar and Dancing Shadows

Golden nectar drips like gold,
Sticky secrets to unfold.
Shadows dance upon the ground,
In our footsteps, joy is found.

We sip the sun, it makes us grin,
Belly laughs erupt within.
Cactus juice and breezy hats,
We're more clumsy than the cats.

Chasing suns with smoothie cups,
Tripping over, tumbling ups.
Our friendship sweet with every sip,
Dripping nectar, not one grip.

As twilight comes, our shadows play,
Bouncing laughter on display.
With sticky hands and joyful hearts,
This summer fun, it never parts.

Fruits of a Sunlit Day

Baskets filled with all things bright,
Cherries popping, pure delight.
Sipping soda, skies are clear,
Jokes about the bees, we cheer.

Warm sun kisses, crispy skin,
Each new taste a silly win.
Lemonade spills, we wipe and laugh,
On the side, a playful calf.

Swinging high, we touch the blue,
Candy dreams with buddy crew.
Hiccups come from all the cheer,
As we toast to summer here.

With fruity bites and giggles small,
Days like these, we have it all.
Life's a festival on our way,
These fruits bring joy to every day.

Sun-Kissed Harvest

Juicy fruits hang from the trees,
A squirrel swipes an apple with ease.
The lemonade stand is out of stock,
While bees dance in a wobbly flock.

Picnics spread on a dappled sheet,
Someone trips on an errant seat.
Sandwiches fly, but we do not care,
Laughter fills the heavy air.

The sun plays tricks, as shadows grow,
A sunburn appears; it has that glow!
There's ice cream melting down my wrist,
I claim it's summer's sweet little kiss.

Whispers of Golden Fields

In fields where daisies freely dance,
A wind-ripped shirt steals my chance.
The hay is stacked like a prankster's tower,
I tumble over in the last hour.

Corn on the cob, I proudly bite,
But sauce erupts in a comical sight.
The chickens chuckle from their perch,
As I try to find the perfect lurch.

Mice in the grass are plotting a scheme,
To nab my sandwich, oh what a dream!
I laugh at the antics, as they do scurry,
This life in the fields is a joyful flurry.

Melodies of a Sun-Baked Day

Sunbeams slip through the window blinds,
Where are my shoes? Where are my minds?
The radio croons, but I dance wrong,
Even my sandwich sings along.

We play catch with a toaster, no doubt,
I toss it high; it starts to pout.
Someone's hidden pickles in the pie,
With every bite, we cannot deny.

Sunscreen lathers like a custard cream,
I glisten like a dream in a hot sunbeam.
The joy of the day is hard to capture,
As bubbles rise in a fizzy rapture.

Nectar on the Breeze

Sweet nectar drips from every flower,
I huff and puff, but oh, what power!
A bee decides to join our dance,
I sway too close, and it takes a chance.

Picnic ants have formed a brigade,
By the crumbs, they've got it made.
I chase them down to reclaim my snack,
With laughter echoing at my back.

Clouds roll in like a comedy show,
I slip on grass, and to the ground I go!
Lemon flavors tickle my tongue,
This wild summer has just begun.

Harvest Moon and Dew-Kissed Soul

Under the harvest moon's bright glow,
Dew-kissed grass tickles my toes.
A raccoon steals pies with flair,
While fireflies dance without a care.

My grandma's holding a water balloon,
Ready to burst with a silvery tune.
Neighbors laugh, chasing each other,
Splashing like kids, oh what a blunder!

The fruit stand's stocked, but it's a race,
To eat the last peach, what a disgrace!
Sticky fingers, big as my heart,
"It's just a snack!" said the thief with art.

Bumblebees buzz, buzzing my ear,
"Hurry, get us honey, we're almost here!"
Laughter erupts like soda pop,
Summer's magic will never stop.

Vibrant Edges of Eternity

Colors splatter like paint on the sky,
Lemons masquerade, oh my, oh my!
Ice cream melts, a pity it goes,
But who needs spoons? We'll eat it with prose!

A sprinkler shoots, it's a water ballet,
Uncle Joe slips — hip, hip, hooray!
Silly giggles burst from the crowd,
As Aunt May's dance is amusingly loud.

I caught a glimpse of a ketchup fight,
Grinning kids, pure delight in sight.
Mom's hollering, "What a mess we make!"
But who can resist a good summer shake?

A butterfly flaps, its wings in bloom,
While dad's BBQ fills all with gloom.
"Is it charcoal or chicken? Please tell me!"
Oh these moments, sweet and free.

The Garden's Embrace

In the garden, veggies like to brawl,
Squash and zucchini take the fall.
Tomatoes giggle, blushing in red,
While carrots plot mischief instead.

Lettuce leaves are fashionistas, you see,
Wearing dew drops, they dance with glee.
"We're so crunchy, hear our crunch!"
Lettuce laughs, "Join us for lunch!"

A bumblebee wears a tiny hat,
Sipping nectar, how about that?
"Buzz off," he hums, "this is my spot!"
"Oh dear," I sigh, "forget what I bought!"

Sunflowers smile 'neath a blue domain,
As gummy worms clap in wild refrain.
Who knew veggies were so bold?
In this garden, laughter unfolds.

Sunlit Strolls and Strawberries

Beneath the sun, we roam so wide,
Strawberries hiding, a sweet surprise.
"Pick me!" they shout, draped in bright red,
It's a berry war, with crumbs spread.

The path is sticky, a joke gone wrong,
Mom's complaining we're singing too long.
But who can resist that juicy delight?
A game of tag takes off, what a sight!

Sun hats sprout like mushrooms, so bold,
A river of giggles starts to unfold.
Dad trips, the cooler's a-foot on the run,
"Did someone say ice cream? I'm still not done!"

A parrot squawks, an unexpected guest,
"Mango madness!" it screams, happy and blessed.
We share our spoils, both funny and bright,
In summer's embrace, everything feels right.

Refreshing Waves of Color

Splashing hues in the sun,
A watermelon won the run.
Lemons dance in a glass so bright,
Sipping laughter, sheer delight.

Sandy toes with jelly beans,
Seagulls squawk in funny scenes.
The ocean laughs with salty cheer,
As I trip on my beachwear, dear.

Beach balls bounce like silly fish,
Floating dreams, it's my only wish.
Got a soda mustache on my face,
Chasing waves at a comical pace.

Cotton candy skies turn to dusk,
While the breeze carries a sweet musk.
Funny hats and ice cream cones,
These moments are my funny bones.

Sweet Serenade of July Nights

Fireflies flicker like popcorn pops,
Underneath the stars, our laughter hops.
Corn on the cob, oh, what a treat,
Dancing ants join our rhythmic beat.

Guitars strum to a sassy tune,
While someone steps on a smelly shoe.
A watermelon provokes a fight,
Seeds flying in the soft moonlight.

Lemonade spills on a giggly face,
As the ice cubes take off in a race.
S'mores get toasted, marshmallows fly,
The night is gifted with a sticky pie.

Laughter bubbles in the warm night air,
Swatting mosquitoes with a wild flair.
Chasing dreams wrapped in a glow,
In the July breeze that steals the show.

Sunlit Flavors on the Tongue

Cherries pop like summer wants,
As my taste buds do little stunts.
Pineapple slush is a playful sip,
While my sunburn demands a trip.

BBQ smoke calls out my name,
Burgers sizzle, it's a flavor game.
With ketchup dribbled down my chin,
I laugh at how it's a win-win.

Hot dogs rolling on the grass,
Under the sun, I dare to pass.
Sweets are scattered, oh what a sight,
A candy fight in the twilight.

Ice cream cones tipped like silly hats,
Kids are giggling, chasing cats.
Every bite's a flavor fling,
In the sun's embrace, we dance and sing.

The Garden's Bounty

Tomatoes red as a fire truck,
Garden gnomes are out of luck.
Zucchini in tennis shoes,
With carrots dancing to their blues.

Herbs are whispering, 'Come and eat!'
Basil's got some funky beat.
Meanwhile, lettuce is feeling shy,
As bees buzz by and say hi.

Cucumbers wear shades in the sun,
While radishes are on the run.
Peas in a pod are having fun,
Playing hopscotch, one by one.

With every crunch and silly sound,
The garden giggles all around.
A picnic feast, so fresh and bright,
Brings us laughter from day to night.

Juicy Moments of July

In July, the sun wears a crown,
Melons explode, juice drips down.
Laughter bursts with each sweet bite,
Sticky fingers in the warm twilight.

Picnics held on a grassy patch,
Where ants march in a perfect batch.
Silly hats and sunburned noses,
We dance with flies, and no one dozes.

Water balloons, a sky-high fling,
Friends take aim, hear the laughter ring.
Every splatter, every splash,
Glorious chaos, a summertime bash.

As the day fades, ice cream calls,
Waffle cones stacked, too big for all.
Drips and giggles, a quirky fate,
In this heat, that's how we celebrate!

Sips of Citrus Delight

A glass with lemon, and oh so sweet,
Chilled on a porch, a perfect treat.
Straws like umbrellas, drinks bubbling high,
Tangled in laughter, oh me, oh my!

Oranges roll like balls in the sun,
Squeezed into juice, oh what fun!
With every sip, a sour face made,
Then bright smiles emerge, worries allayed.

Neighbors gather, cheers fill the air,
Lime wedges squirted without a care.
Jokes fly faster than drinks we consume,
Time seems to linger, in this sunny room.

As the sun dips low, glasses we raise,
To the citrus cheer and delightful days.
With sticky fingers and zesty grins,
Our hearts are light, where the laughter begins!

Lush Berries at Dusk

Beneath the bushes, a berry hunt,
Fingers stained, oh, what a stunt!
Plump and juicy, oh so divine,
Raspberry giggles, we sip on wine.

Blueberry stains on a white dress fair,
"Oops!" I shout, laughter fills the air.
Chasing dreams with each juicy scoop,
Making messes in our berry troop.

Strawberries tossed in a sticky bowl,
Whipped cream clouds, we lose control.
A race to see who can make the most,
Silly faces while we gleefully boast.

As dusk embraces, flavors collide,
In this berry patch, we take a ride.
With fruity laughter and stained delights,
Under starry skies, we share our bites!

The Warmth of Ripened Dreams

In the garden, where tomatoes swing,
Laughter echoes, oh what a fling!
Next to zucchinis that seem to grow,
Under bright sunlight, our faces glow.

With every misstep, a funny scene,
Cucumbers slip, oh how they glean!
Hidden treasures in muddy ground,
Giggles erupt with every round.

Pineapple hats and peppers as bling,
We dance around to a comical fling.
A recipe book filled with scribbles and stains,
Creating chaos in summer's veins.

As dusk settles, we feast on our dreams,
A mix of flavors and silly schemes.
Among the warmth, we laugh and play,
In this summer's garden, we find our way!

Cool Mornings and Warm Hearts

The sun peeks in with a sleepy yawn,
Birds chirp loudly like a tiny dawn.
Coffee spills, a dance on the floor,
Laughter erupts, we always want more.

The breeze tickles, like a playful tease,
Flip-flops flop as we skip with ease.
Butterflies flutter in a chaotic race,
We've all got grins that no one can erase.

Grandma's cookies, the hot-off-the-grill,
Giggling children with their stubborn will.
Water balloons ready for a sneak attack,
Watch out, my friend—no turning back!

Breezy hats that fly with a twist,
We chase them down, oh, how could we miss?
Cool mornings like these, we cherish the art,
Of silly moments that warm every heart.

Vibrant Market Days and Fleeting Glances

Baskets piled high, colors collide,
Strawberries flirt like they're on a ride.
Pickles and jams in a curious dance,
Caught in a glance, oh what a chance!

Churros and laughter fill the bright air,
A sudden splash from a juice stand scare.
We juggle our treasures, what a delight!
Kite strings tugging, a whimsical flight.

Shoppers collide in a comedy scene,
"Excuse me!" "Oops!" as we vie for the green.
Bargains and banter, a casual spree,
With grocery carts, we whirl like the sea.

The sun dips low, and the stalls begin close,
But memories linger like sweet, sticky prose.
What a fine day of dizzying laughs,
We'll come back again—for more silly crafts!

Cotton Candy Skies at Fairgrounds

Fluffy clouds swirl like candy on air,
We chase the rides without a care.
Tickets flutter like they're dancing away,
While cotton candy sparks our play.

Bumper cars bump, giggles escape,
A giant slide makes a wild shape.
Laughter erupts, the carousel spins,
As each silly moment somehow begins.

Sticky fingers, who took my prize?
A fortune teller with glittery eyes.
Silly hats bobbing, we join in the throng,
Singing off-key to our favorite song.

Night falls gently, lights start to beam,
Fireworks burst—what a wild dream!
Every squeal and shriek in the night,
Cotton candy skies, oh what a sight!

Laughter Echoes Under the Canopy

Under the trees, with shade so sweet,
Picnics spread out, what a treat!
Sandwiches wobble, chips take a dive,
It's all about joy—and the bees arrive.

Frisbees fly, landing with a plop,
Who knew fun could make us swap?
Spritz the dog, water's a laugh,
A treasure trove of mischief and craft.

Granny's old blanket is full of tales,
Of glorious fails and epic gales.
We recount the quirks of past summer glee,
With every chuckle, it's just you and me.

As shadows fade and daylight sighs,
The echo of fun will never die.
With laughter weaving through branches and leaves,
Under the canopy, our hearts believe.

A Bite of Radiance

The sun spilled juice on the grass,
A slip and slide for the ants.
Sips of nectar from marigold cups,
Dancing bees in their fragrant pants.

Picnics with cheese that squeaks out loud,
Watermelons giggle as they roll.
Crumbs of cookies scatter like seeds,
Even the sun seems to lose control.

Chasing shadows, we skip past the heat,
Kites flutter, connect like lost friends.
Ice cream drips down with a splash and a plop,
Oh summer days, where the fun just extends.

Notes of laughter from the garden's best,
Tomatoes blush, but are they in jest?
With every bite, we grow a little bright,
A humorous feast under a golden light.

Laughter in a Lemonade Glass

Sippin' sunshine in a glass,
It tickles the nose, oh what a blast!
Add a twist of lime and some giggles too,
We're on a citrus journey, just me and you.

Cups clink together, rumbles of fun,
As we swirl the sweetness, who's got the run?
Bee in the drink, do we call him Fred?
He's buzzing around, got lemon dreams in his head.

Straws get tangled, a slippery mess,
Slurping our laughs, who needs the stress?
A splash from a wave of bright yellow cheer,
Chasing worries, we hold summer near.

Sippin' and spillin', we ride on this wave,
A toast to the laughter that we all crave.
Under the sun, we dance and we sway,
Lemonade bliss, we're here to play.

Harvesting Sunshine

Swinging at dusk, the swing set creaks,
Glimmers of daylight on sunshine peaks.
Cherries pop with a plump little burst,
Sneaky squirrels, they're always the worst.

Grass stains on knees, laughter too loud,
We're crafting mischief, like kids allowed.
Berries squished on fingers and toes,
Messy delights, that's how summer goes.

Keep an eye out for runaway pies,
Even the sky is wearing surprise.
Flip-flops flap like they're stuck on a tune,
While we skate on sidewalks beneath the full moon.

Gathering memories, like jars full of light,
These moments of joy, oh, what a sight!
With daisies in hair, let's giggle along,
Harvesting sunshine, where we all belong.

Delectable Days in July

Oh July, how you tantalize,
With corn on the cob and summer pies.
A sudden rain, like nature's joke,
We dance 'round puddles with strawberry smoke.

Grilling delights that sizzle and pop,
While ants do the polka, forget the mop!
Hot dogs doing the cha-cha, oh my,
Watch them spin, as the condiments fly.

Margins of laughter scribbled on sand,
And sunburned noses, oh isn't it grand?
We fashion our dreams into kites that can soar,
And giggle till our sides feel sore.

So here's to the days where the fun never dies,
With flavors of summer under wide-open skies.
Let's savor the moments, both silly and bright,
Delectable days, oh what pure delight!

Vibrant Flavors of Dusk

Underneath the twilight sky,
Lemonade spills, oh my, oh my!
Ice-cream cones dripping down,
Sticky fingers in every town.

Fireflies dance, a twinkling parade,
Chasing them down, we can't be swayed!
Cotton candy wisps float by,
Like fluffy dreams that make us sigh.

In the park, each bite's a delight,
Churros hot, just out of sight!
Neighbors laugh and whimsical cheer,
Who knew sweet moments could appear?

As the sun sinks, the giggles grow,
All our antics put on a show!
With flavors bold and skies that blush,
We savor chaos in a summer rush.

Savoring Moments of Golden Hour

Juicy burgers on the grill,
Everyone's got their mouth to fill!
Pickles dancing, oh what a sight,
Buns taking flights into the night!

Corn on the cob, buttered and dripped,
Faces smeared with every little nib.
Laughter rings, a silly affair,
Ketchup fights – but who would dare?

Blazing stars begin to peek,
S'mores melting, they're all unique!
Chocolate rivers, marshmallow streams,
We gobble up our sticky dreams.

Golden hour, laughter's spell,
Crazy flavors we all can't quell!
In this moment, nothing's missed,
Memories wrapped in a sugary twist.

Floating on a Watermelon Wave

Watermelon slices, what a surprise,
Fashionable hats and goofy eyes!
Juicy drips down our chins and necks,
Boat-shaped floats, perfect for pecks.

Splashing about, a slippery game,
In this sea of flavors, we're never the same!
Giggling kids, all squeals and laughter,
The sun's a star, happily after.

With every bite, we taste the sun,
Making memories, oh what fun!
Juice oozes, and oh, what a sight,
Our fruity kingdom, feels just right!

Underneath the bright blue dome,
Each float's a slice of summer's foam.
In our hearts, it's wild and loud,
Floating on waves, we're truly proud.

Sparkling Skies, Juicy Delights

Twinkling lights, a late-night feast,
Around the table, we laugh, at least!
Pineapple skewers, grilled just so,
Watch out, someone steals the show!

Fizzling drinks in glassy jars,
Straws like rockets, aiming for stars!
Popcorn tosses, cheers ignite,
Funny faces, all in delight.

Berry picking, who can resist?
Hands all stained, well that's the gist!
Pies cooling down, a sweet parade,
Taste test fields, this summer's made!

Every sip, a burst of bright,
While the rooftops light the night.
In our hearts, we keep the thrills,
Juicy delights, and laughter spills!

An Orchard of Bliss

In the orchard, laughter grows,
Where tree branches dance and doze.
Bees buzzing tales of sticky treat,
Juicy fruits make life so sweet.

With a bite, surprise and glee,
Squirrels laugh, a cheeky spree.
Melon balls in a caper's toss,
Mismatched socks highlight the gloss.

Old sneakers on the grass do sway,
Like tiny kites that want to play.
A plump peach slips, oh what a mess!
Rolling laughter, summer's best!

Chocolate stains on every cheek,
Giggling kids all freeze to peek.
Syrupy fingers wave from the tree,
"Pass the lemonade, whee!"

Sunset Cherries

Cherries gleam like little suns,
As we chase each other for fun.
With each bite, a bright red blush,
While we giggle in a mad rush.

Sticky faces, wild and free,
Pit spitting contests, glee!
"Who can launch it past the dog?"
His bewildered face, a comic fog.

On the porch, two pals dispute,
Which fruit brings a tastier loot?
"A grape's just a cherry with an 'accident'!"
With laughter echoing, oh what fun we spent!

At twilight, the sky burns bright,
Chucking cherry pits feels just right.
Our summer days, a wild spree,
Where we crown cherries as the key!

Flavors of Freedom

Ice cream drips down my chin,
As I race 'gainst the breeze with a grin.
Rainbow sprinkles like confetti fall,
With each lick, I have a ball!

Fudge fountains spray our shoes,
Sticky toes, we can't refuse.
Jumping puddles, flavors collide,
Who knew giggles could be our guide?

Bouncing out of a melting cone,
We ask the sun to chill our tone.
Popcorn clouds and caramel skies,
We slurp soda with buddy ties.

Freedom flavors, wild and bold,
In summer's tale, we are told.
From syrupy youth, we take a slice,
In the land of giggles, life's a paradise!

Ocean Breeze

Waves crash, giggles rise so high,
Seagulls plot with a funny eye.
Sand castles stand like royal halls,
While ice cream drips like sweet waterfalls.

Surfboards lined, just for sway,
"Dude, did you bring the snacks today?"
Belly flops make spectators cheer,
Splash battles echo summer's leer.

Seashell treasures with stuck-on sand,
As we frolic hand in hand.
Sandy notes on a boardwalk stroll,
"Catch that frisbee, take control!"

At twilight, the sunset ignites,
With marshmallow dreams and kite flights.
Ocean breeze, a whiff of bliss,
Where laughter swims and joy exists!

Berry Bliss

Berries piled high for a feast,
Juice-stained fingers, feeling beast!
Blueberry headbands, misfit crew,
Squishing fruits, what's new with you?

Raspberries revolt, a squishy combat,
"Dodge this!" and "Let's battle that!"
As strawberries play dress-up game,
Silly hats, who takes the fame?

Under bushes, secrets hide,
A fruity treasure we'll abide.
With every squirt, a giggle flies,
Summer's joy beneath the skies.

When it's time to clean the floor,
Messy faces call for more!
With berry bliss, our hearts take flight,
A summer tale, a pure delight!

Balmy Nights of Endless Stars

Under the sky, the crickets sing,
We dance with shadows, let joy take wing.
Bubbles pop like summer's flair,
Who knew mosquitoes could be such a pair?

Lemonade fountains flow and spill,
Tommy's sip ends in a giddy thrill.
Jumping in pools with a belly flop,
Splashing all around, no chance to stop!

Fireflies twinkle, stars look down,
We giggle so hard, tripping on the crown.
Is that a comet or just Dad's snore?
All night long, we keep asking for more!

The moon's a balloon, round and fat,
We play hide and seek with the neighborhood cat.
Each giggle echoes, under the night,
In these balmy moments, all feels just right.

The Aroma of Freshly Cut Grass

A symphony hums with each slice and chop,
Dad sneezes loud, and then we all stop.
Perfumed blades dance, green and bright,
While bugs conspire, a real fly fight!

We roll down hills, through the emerald sea,
Grass stains on knees—a badge we foresee.
Socks on our hands, we perform a grand play,
Slipping and sliding, yelling hooray!

Joyful chaos, we build a fort,
From clippings tall, what a silly sport!
But oh! The mower makes its buzzing sound,
We scatter like ants when danger's around!

An aroma rich like Mom's baking bread,
But we've just mowed, our mischief is spread.
In this green kingdom, we feel like kings,
Amidst all the laughter, anticipation springs.

Juicy Secrets in the Orchard

In the orchard, we find treasures bright,
Cherries hide, and they're quite a sight!
We climb the trees with shoes that slip,
Face full of juice, it's a morning trip!

Giggles erupt as Dad starts to climb,
Plucking apples while singing a rhyme.
"Watch for bees!" he shouts from above,
As we dodge with laughter, nothing but love!

The ground is a mess, and so are we,
Stains on our shirts—from fruit jubilee.
"Who threw that peach?" echoes through the air,
It's a juicy war! We don't have a care.

In the shade of the trees, we plot our next raid,
Souring the sweetness and making parade.
With bites, we declare, "This one's the best!"
Creating juicy secrets, summer's funny jest!

Savoring Sunlit Memories

Sunshine spills like syrup on toast,
We chase the ice cream truck, that's our boast.
Dripping cones and giggles many,
Who knew sprinkles could be so zany?

Burgers sizzle on the grill, what a sound,
Dad flips them high, the crowd astound.
Ketchup wars erupt and fly,
Catching kids laugh, oh me, oh my!

Tricycles zoom in a mad parade,
Sidewalk chalk reveals our escapade.
Drawing the sun with shades too bright,
As we bask under the glow of light.

Couch forts made from sunbeam lines,
Whispering secrets over lemonade pines.
Locked in these moments, we snatch our glee,
Savoring memories, so sweet and free!

www.ingramcontent.com/pod-product-compliance
Lightning Source LLC
Chambersburg PA
CBHW070310120526
44590CB00017B/2609